ALL ABOUT BREEDING
LOVEBIRDS

ALL ABOUT BREEDING
LOVEBIRDS

MERVIN F. ROBERTS

Photography: Glen S. Axelrod, 14, 36, 42, 61, 65, 90 (top). Herbert R. Axelrod, 6, 15, 19, 20, 26, 34, 39, 41, 43, 46, 72, 74 (bottom), 83, 86, 87, 90 (bottom), 91. Kerry V. Donnelly, 49, 52, 92. Michael Gilroy, frontis, 10, 18, 71, 79, 82, 94-5. Barbara Kotlar, 54. Harry Lacey, 8. H. Reinhard, 7, 22, 27, 78. Mervin F. Roberts, 35 (top), 50, 51, 55, 58, 59, 62, 63, 67, 70. Courtesy San Diego Zoo, 23, 30, 31, 74 (top). Tony Silva, 35 (bottom), 38, 75. Courtesy Vogelpark Walsrode, 80. Matthew M. Vriends, 66.

Frontis. A pair of Fischer's Lovebirds. Characteristic of all the lovebird species with white eye rings is their lack of sexual dimorphism; that is to say, males and females look alike.

Distributed in the UNITED STATES by T.F.H. Publications, Inc., 211 West Sylvania Avenue, Neptune City, NJ 07753; in CANADA by H & L Pet Supplies Inc., 27 Kingston Crescent, Kitchener, Ontario N2B 2T6; Rolf C. Hagen Ltd., 3225 Sartelon Street, Montreal 382 Quebec; in ENGLAND by T.F.H. (Great Britain) Ltd., 11 Ormside Way, Holmethorpe Industrial Estate, Redhill, Surrey RH1 2PX; in AUSTRALIA AND THE SOUTH PACIFIC by T.F.H. (Australia) Pty. Ltd., Box 149, Brookvale 2100 N.S.W., Australia; in NEW ZEALAND by Ross Haines & Son, Ltd., 18 Monmouth Street, Grey Lynn, Auckland 2 New Zealand; in SINGAPORE AND MALAYSIA by MPH Distributors Pte., 71-77 Stamford Road, Singapore 0617; in the PHILIPPINES by Bio-Research, 5 Lippay Street, San Lorenzo Village, Makati, Rizal; in SOUTH AFRICA by Multipet Pty. Ltd., 30 Turners Avenue, Durban 4001. Published by T.F.H. Publications Inc., Ltd., the British Crown Colony of Hong Kong.

Contents

Pairs of lovebirds, such as the Peach-faced Lovebirds (*above*) and the Masked Lovebirds (*opposite*), often can be seen snuggling up to each other. They frequently chatter to themselves and kiss and preen each other with great devotion.

The easy-to-breed lovebird species unfortunately are often the most difficult to sex, as is the case with this Masked Lovebird pair.

Introduction

The major thrust in this book is to help you to breed love-birds. It is important to realize that although some love-bird varieties have been studied and bred in cages since 1860, it is extremely unlikely that any *pure* stock from 1860 is alive today. Imports over the years have been introduced into aviaries, so no one today can absolutely guarantee a pedigree going back more than a few decades.

This means that we are dealing with *relatively* wild birds. Remember that pigeons, ducks, chickens, canaries, and geese have been bred domestically for centuries. Charles Darwin in 1859 wrote of pigeons domesticated in Egypt five thousand years ago, and that's a long time ago. Chickens were developed from their wild Indian progenitors also over the course of several thousand years. Even canaries have been kept in cages for four hundred years. A flock of domestic geese is said to have warned a Roman garrison of invaders in 390 B.C.

So, with a bird that takes nearly a year to reproduce itself, just one-hundred-and-twenty-odd years of domestication with certain backcrosses to wild stock is not a very long time. This suggests that a breeder seeking success is well advised to adjust to the wild bird's habits rather than to attempt to manipulate the birds to fit into captivity.

The lovebird species best suited to beginners are the least expensive. That's reasonable when you reflect on it—other breeders have also found them easy to propagate. So, for starters, no matter how much money you can afford to invest in lovebirds, start with a high-quality pair of an inexpensive species. That was easy to write, but it may be

From the mass of color and sea of faces (*above*), one can isolate a single Fischer's Lovebird (*opposite*) to appreciate more closely the beauty of its brightly-colored plumage.

difficult to accomplish. You may want to pay a premium for a guaranteed breeding pair, or you may decide to start with six juveniles and let them pair up. The chance of getting at least one pair is better than 95% if you choose six birds at random. The problem, if you don't already know, is that the "easy-to-breed" lovebirds are sexually monomorphic. That is, both sexes look alike, or nearly so.

The "easiest" of the lovebirds is probably the Peach-faced, followed by the Nyasa, Masked, Fischer's, and Black-cheeked, in no particular order. (The last four named are, by some rules of classification, all members of the same species—more about that later.)

A pair of lovebirds capable of reproducing themselves could cost less than the cage necessary to house them and their progeny. This should tell you something. Simply put, breeding lovebirds is not difficult for them or for you. Of course, they are not as common or as hardy as the pigeons that nest in an abandoned barn or under a railroad trestle; but in their African homeland, many species of lovebirds are quite plentiful, in their relatively restricted ranges.

They live a long time in captivity. A pair can produce three clutches of four babies each, per year. Youngsters from eggs laid on the first of June will hatch, grow, mature, mate, nest, and produce fertile eggs by or before the following May.

A lovebird can live a decade or more without being handled or medicated in any way. Lovebirds are easy to feed, tolerant of relatively wide fluctuations in climate, and resistant to most disease; hence they are, to many bird keepers, most desirable birds.

If you are interested in genetics or in systematic classification, this group of birds is for you, since there are many color varieties already available. Also, there has been a good deal of hybridizing among the species, providing an ongoing challenge for some aviculturists. By contrast, although Budgerigars and Cockatiels are well endowed with color varieties, neither offer the opportunities afforded by hybridization.

If the lovebird bug has bitten you, the best advice you can follow is to read as much as you can *before* you try to innovate. The second best advice is to join the African Lovebird Society, Box 142, San Marcos, California 92069.

Who's Who?

You can keep and enjoy and even breed lovebirds without knowing anything contained in this chapter. But, if you wish to settle old arguments and perhaps start some new ones, read on. If you wish simply to care for your birds and enjoy them, skip this and go on to the next chapter.

Natural history is full of complications and confusions. This is a Universal Truth; we all must learn to live with it. Fortunately, as we pursue natural history, we find that birds are relatively easy to study. Granted, their fossil record is sketchy and will probably remain so because of their frail bones. But living birds are easy to find, easy to observe, easy to collect, easy to preserve, and easy to examine. Their behavior, diet, anatomy, and distribution all provide clues to their location on the Tree of Life.

Aves is the scientific name for the class of birds, which includes all warm-blooded, egg-laying, feathered creatures. Some of their features are reptilian and some are mammalian. This much, everyone should agree, is easy, with no complications and no confusions.

Members of the Psittaciformes, the order of parrots, are characterized by hooked bills, two toes pointing forward and two backward, a fleshy cere at the base of the bill, special feathers called powder downs, and a movable upper mandible, not rigidly attached to the skull. Parrots use their bills to aid in climbing, and they hold their food with their feet—these features also help set them apart. Now things get a little complicated. The features which distinguish parrots are not exclusively limited to parrots. Hawks and owls also are hook-billed. Woodpeckers, cuckoos, turacos, barbets, and owls also have but two of

There are a number of color varieties (mutations) of the Peach-faced Lovebird that have occurred in captivity, including Dutch Blue (*above*) and Lutino and White (*opposite*).

their four toes pointing forward. Herons, too, have powder downs. Also, the movable upper mandible is not unique to parrots. On the other hand, herons have long, straight bills; owls look forward; and hawks lack gravel-filled gizzards. But when the chips are down, we know a parrot when we see one. Of course, there is that one rare, nocturnal, flightless New Zealand parrot whose eyes, like owls', do face forward, but it will soon be extinct, and that should help tidy up the chart.

Having cleared the hurdles of class (easy), and order (a bit sticky), we find that the families of parrots are positively confusing. Perhaps, In The Beginning, our Creator did not design from a tidy chart. There are discontinuities; the branches of the Tree of Life are twisted. Various experts propose various arrangements. The following is that of Joseph M. Forshaw (*Parrots of the World*), who separates the parrots (Psittaciformes) into three families:

> Lories (Loriidae)—these birds eat pollen and nectar; their tongues are especially adapted for this special diet.

> Cockatoos (Cacatuidae)—these are the crested parrots; they spend their time in trees.

> All other parrots (Psittacidae)—none have tongues adapted for pollen, and none have erectile crests. In this family we find the subfamily Psittacinae, which encompasses the lovebirds, genus *Agapornis*.

Recognized experts agree that all the lovebirds are members of this one genus. The confusion compounds at the species level. Some forms of lovebird are granted a species designation, while others are relegated to subspecies, or race. Our Creator never ordained in writing that experts were required to agree; with lovebirds especially, few do.

So then, what is a lovebird? This much we know; it is a short-tailed African parrot, brightly colored, and about seven inches long. Its head is relatively broad, and it has a relatively large beak. Mated pairs sometimes bicker and fight. They also frequently perch closely and preen each other. Some people call that love. Far be it from me to define love; I can't even define species.

What else causes us to lump these little parrots together as lovebirds? Well, their behavior is an important criterion. This genus includes forms which carry nesting material by tucking it under their feathers—not all, but some do it. They build nests or nest pads—not all, but some do it. Their ability to interbreed is another criterion. In captivity they have little trouble hybridizing to produce fertile offspring—not all, but again, some do it.

In addition to their behavior and their ability to interbreed and their appearance, taxonomists also take note of their geographical distribution and the chemical and microscopic constitution of their tissues.

Before you begin to think you know what's going on, consider the Mallophaga. These are parasitic lice found on the feathers and skin of birds. Now, Mallophaga are, among themselves, extremely specialized, so that certain forms of these lice are limited to certain birds. So, far-fetched as it may seem, some scientists now use these lowly lice to aid in determining the relationships between bird species.

Do scientific names awe you or snow you, or do they just turn you off? Did you ever say, "Oh, that Latin-name stuff is not for me"? Well, look carefully at the scientific name of the genus of lovebirds. It is *Agapornis*, and that's not Latin, it's Greek! Once you see how, in 1836, Selby coined the compound, the awesomeness is unveiled and the designation makes simple, straightforward sense. *Agape* is the Greek word for love. *Orni* is also Greek; it refers to birds (that's how we come to call the study of birds *orni*thology). So *Agape* + *ornis* = *Agapornis*, the genus of lovebirds. Eureka!

Peach-faced Lovebirds, characterized by their pinkish-red faces and horn-colored beaks (*above*), are hardy, willing breeders; however, like the four white-eye-ring species, they are sexually monomorphic (it is difficult to differentiate males from females). The Peach-faced cock (*opposite*) relishes an unripe cherry while his mate looks on.

Regardless of the lovebird species you choose to breed or the source from which you purchase your birds, be absolutely certain that you select strong, healthy stock.

Species, Hybrids, Varieties

SPECIES

Before you can know how many species of lovebirds there are, you must decide what a species is. This is not easy. As I mentioned previously, I don't know. I used to think I knew, but as I get older I wonder. If you are an ordinary take-it-or-leave-it person, I advise you not to get too deeply involved. This study has driven great minds to the bottle and has made enemies of those who had been friends. So I suggest you fight your way through this chapter and then leave it with an open mind; better informed perhaps, but not dogmatic, because this isn't dogma. It is just an attempt by ordinary mortals to get a handle on things.

One old, respected definition of a species is this: a population in which the individuals resemble each other (sexual and age differences excepted) and in which the offspring are fertile and resemble their parents.

Another definition puts more emphasis on the geographic limits of this population. Isolated on an island or across a river or behind a range of mountains or by a discontinuity in the food supply, a group of animals become more like each other and less like those that are located elsewhere. The finches which Darwin described on the Galapagos Islands are a good example. Other definitions rely more on subtle differences in the chemistry of tissue proteins or in the arrangement of the microscopic chromosomes found in every cell. After nailing down a species,

The red feathering around the eyes of the cock Black-winged Love-bird (*above*) contrasts with the white (unfeathered) eye ring of the Blue and Yellow Masked Lovebirds (*opposite*).

some taxonomists then consider subspecies and races. This gets more and more sticky.

Let's look at a list; maybe it will help. The names given here follow *Parrots of the World* by Forshaw and Cooper.

An easy way to group lovebirds distinguishes between those that have white eye rings and those that don't. Besides appearance, the two groups have other common characteristics, as you'll see.

WITHOUT WHITE EYE RINGS:

Gray-headed Lovebird (*Agapornis cana*). *Distinguishing features:* Gray-headed male, green-headed female. Horn-colored bill. *Habit notes:* High-strung. Nests in holes in trees. Female carries nesting material in body feathers.

Red-faced Lovebird (*Agapornis pullaria*). *Distinguishing features:* Red face on male, red bill; female has less intense red. *Habit notes:* Eats mealworms. Nests in the mud structures made by arboreal termites. Female carries nesting material in body feathers.

Black-winged Lovebird (*Agapornis taranta*). *Distinguishing features:* Male has red on forehead and around eyes; female has no red feathers. Red bill. *Habit notes:* Eats juniper seeds. Bickers. Favors a small cavity for nesting. Female carries nesting material in body feathers.

Black-collared Lovebird (*Agapornis swinderniana*). *Distinguishing features:* Black collar, black bill. Sexes alike. *Habit notes:* Eats figs. Lives in high trees. Nesting habits not known.

Peach-faced Lovebird (*Agapornis roseicollis*). *Distinguishing features:* Peach-colored face, horn-colored bill. Sexes alike. *Habit notes:* Scrappy. Opportunistic nester—in cavities, crevices, deserted nests of other birds. Female carries nesting material in feathers of lower back and rump.

The white-eye-ring lovebirds show even more similarity

among themselves—there are no behavior characteristics that distinguish one from another.

Masked Lovebird (*Agapornis personata*). *Distinguishing features:* Black head, red bill. Sexes alike.

Fischer's Lovebird (*Agapornis fischeri*). *Distinguishing features:* Breast, neck, and head orange-red. Red bill. Sexes alike.

Nyasa Lovebird (*Agapornis lilianae*). *Distinguishing features:* Like Fischer's, but less intense orange-red. Sexes alike.

Black-cheeked Lovebird (*Agapornis nigrigenis*). *Distinguishing features:* Black cheeks, rose bill. Sexes alike.

Habit notes: Avid bathers. Opportunistic nesters—in cavities, crevices, deserted nests of other birds. Females carry nesting material in the bill.

You can understand why all the white-eye-ring forms are considered by some authorities to be subspecies of *Agapornis personata*. If that is how you wish to lump them, then their scientific names would look like this:

Masked: *Agapornis personata personata*
Nyasa: *A. personata lilianae*
Black-cheeked: *A. personata nigrigenis*
Fischer's: *A. personata fischeri*

HYBRIDS

A hybrid, according to one of the popular and traditional definitions, is an offspring from the union of different species. The mule and hinny are hybrids born of the union between horse and ass. The liger and tigon derive from the lion-tiger cross. These hybrids are usually sterile, but in some instances, the hybrids are even easier to propagate than their parents were. When it comes to lovebirds, many hybrid offspring are fertile.

Since not all lovebirds are known to hybridize, the picture is a little complicated. Let's take a quick look at the crosses which have been achieved and recognized to date.

Fischer's Lovebirds (*above*) and Nyasa Lovebirds (*opposite*) have similar red-orange coloring on the forehead, chin, and throat. In Fischer's, though, this color is more intense and extends onto the cheeks as well; additionally, there is a collar of yellow extending onto the upper breast, which is not found in the Nyasa.

This chart was derived from as much source material as I could uncover. It is one easy thing to claim a hybrid; it is far more difficult to prove the claim. Note that the convention in describing hybrid crosses is to list the male first, that is, to the left of the "x."

Gray-headed	— None known
Red-faced	— None known
Black-winged	x Masked
Black-collared	— None known
Peach-faced	x Masked Fischer's Nyasa Black-cheeked
Masked	x Fischer's Nyasa Black-cheeked Peach-faced
Fischer's	x Masked Nyasa Black-cheeked Peach-faced
Nyasa	x Masked Fischer's Black-cheeked
Black-cheeked	x Masked Nyasa

You can see that not all the crosses work in both directions, and some we would expect to find haven't been accomplished—that is the fun and the challenge of it.

One additional aspect of captive-bred lovebird identification deserving attention here is that breeding records don't necessarily accompany the birds. Hybrids get mixed into the population of birds which are constantly being purchased, traded, given as gifts, stolen, and eventually mated and bred. Is your Peach-faced an absolutely purebred Peach-faced? I doubt if anyone can tell. If it looks most like a Peach-faced, then that is what it will be called. Granted, that's not very scientific.

VARIETIES

A mutant is the product of a genetic "accident." If a mutant has two heads, we call it a freak. If the "accident" causes a slight color or pattern change, we may notice it and then breed from that individual in order to establish a population of this new variety.

Mutants in nature are the building blocks of Darwin's theory of evolution through natural selection. Every mutation is a *random* thing. Some are good and some are bad for their bearers. The mutant organism is larger or smaller or weaker or stronger or noisier or quieter or colored differently or more or less resistant to heat or cold or whatever. As a result, it may fall by the wayside, or it may thrive and be especially successful in reproducing offspring which also have this trait. In captivity, natural selection is less of a factor for survival. *We* do the selecting, and *we* choose the individuals which are to mate and reproduce themselves.

For example, albinos are mutants, and most albinos in wild populations of birds or fishes or mammals or reptiles don't survive or thrive because they are usually frail and have poor vision and no protective coloration (outside the snow belt). Although we know of captive albino raccoons and mice and rabbits and snakes and ferrets and birds, we don't know of thriving wild populations of albinos. The same goes for lutinos and pieds and many other color varieties of finches, canaries, budgies, poultry, and, of course, lovebirds.

Let's look at the color varieties of lovebirds. Again we will not pay strict attention to the species, since Mother Nature hasn't taken a firm, hard line in this matter.

Black-collared, Black-cheeked—None known.

Black-winged — Cinnamon.

Gray-headed — None known. The gray head of the male may be more or less lavender, but this may be a matter of diet.

Red-faced — Lutino.

Peach-faced — Lutino, Yellow, Pied, Blue, Dark Green, White.

Masked — Blue, Yellow, White.

Fischer's — Blue.

Nyasa — Lutino.

A Black-cheeked Lovebird (*above*) and a Red-faced Lovebird (*opposite*). Unlike the other eight lovebird species, the Red-faced in the wild builds its nest in arboreal termite mounds.

This list is incomplete—no list can be completed unless the species is extinct. Furthermore, I am sure I missed many. You should go on in your reading to *Lovebirds and Related Parrots* by George A. Smith. After Smith, I suggest that you read *Lovebirds and their Color Mutations* by Jim Hayward.

And when you think you have caught up with what is already known, you should join the African Lovebird Society and/or you should become a member of the nearest avicultural society—the list of these clubs is published in *American Cage-Bird Magazine* every month.

Incidentally, you should subscribe to the American Cage-Bird Magazine (3449 N. Western Ave., Chicago, Illinois 60618). This monthly is the premier U.S. publication for the cage-bird fancy. The contributing editors are all recognized experts, and the advertising is also useful to anyone who keeps birds. For an example of the editorial content, look at the February and March 1981 issues. A wonderfully informative two-part article by Dr. Stephen Buggie is entitled "Lovebirds of the Zambian Bush," and the references alone will keep you and your local librarian busy for a long time.

Nutrition

FOOD

Lovebirds in Africa and crows in North America have some things in common. In both places, farmers have no great love for them, but some people do keep them as pets. Lovebirds, like crows, often appear at a planted field and go through it, consuming a great deal and damaging still more. Another aspect of the eating habits of both is that they have cosmopolitan tastes. Both will eat many fruits and vegetables. Some lovebirds eat mealworms; likewise, crows follow the plow for grubs. Lovebirds may eat a bit of meat or pick at a bone from time to time; so also with crows. Of course, they both eat many grains.

After as long as a century of domestication for some species and perhaps some hybridization, it seems appropriate to first briefly mention the foods lovebirds are known to eat in the wild and then to go on to discuss the diets which have proven successful for them in captivity.

Red-faced—grass seed, millet, canary, morning-glory leaves, guavas, figs, berries.
Gray-headed—rice, millet.
Black-winged—juniper seeds, euphorbia seeds, green food, fruit, figs.
Black-collared—strangler figs, seeds, insects.
Peach-faced—millet, small seeds, maize, berries.
Masked—cereal crops, millet.
Fischer's—millet, maize.
Nyasa—seeds, buds, millet.
Black-cheeked—seeds, fruits, berries, buds.

As you can see, this list is loose and indefinite. It surely contains gaps and perhaps it is not entirely accurate, but it is the best we have right now, so make the most of it.

Lovebirds are basically seedeaters, but they need a variety of foods in their diet (*above*). Uneaten food should be removed each day so that it does not have a chance to spoil. Nestlings (*opposite, above*) are fed soft, partially digested food by their parents, but orphaned or hand-reared youngsters (*opposite, below*) can be fed a gruel-like rearing food until they mature and learn to hull seeds.

Millet spray is always a favorite treat among lovebirds kept in both aviaries and cages.

Lovebirds will not overeat, nor will they likely eat something which is not good for them; if you show generosity, imagination, and patience, your birds will show you what they thrive on while you continue to offer variety. The point of a variety of foods to caged birds is that it protects them against malnutrition caused by the lack of trace elements, obscure vitamins, or amino acids. Most creatures will crave what they lack. Even if the usual food source of this substance is lacking in their diet, there is a good chance they will accept a substitute food in order to get that missing ingredient. One example of this is, of course, the cuttlebone. No wild lovebird ever saw a cuttlefish—we can be sure of that—but cuttlebone is an excellent source of calcium, which lovebirds do crave and consume.

Raw, fresh, wild figs are not something you will find in your neighborhood supermarket or even in any pet shop I have visited, but since we know that some lovebird species eat them in the wild, we should certainly offer figs to our caged birds. Millet soaked in fig juice has also been suggested for lovebirds; it wouldn't hurt to try.

Your pet lovebird, or two or three, will do well on the seed mix available from your pet shop and supplements from the kitchen and garden. If you keep more than a pair and their young offspring, this is surely the route to take. When your collection amounts to more than a half-dozen birds, it is time to buy bagged mixes or even to mix your own.

You have two problems. The first—and this is relatively easy—is to find and provide a nourishing and wholesome diet for your lovebirds. The second is usually infinitely more difficult: you must get the birds to eat it. Often you will offer a food that you know is good for your lovebirds, and it will be ignored, rejected, disdained. Only after repeated offerings will your birds eat apple or banana or dandelion greens or whatever, yet you know of dozens of fanciers who have fed hundreds of birds these very things for decades! Well, that is part of the challenge.

The following items should all be included in a diet for lovebirds:

Millet—white, yellow, and red. This is an important ingredient of most lovebird diets.

After a rest, a lovebird like this Peach-faced (*above*) will often stretch its wings. Lovebirds are hardy birds and need plenty of room for exercise. If several pairs are kept, it makes sense to house them in an aviary, with each breeding pair confined to its own flight (*opposite, above*). Provide each pair with two nest boxes (*opposite, below*); these can easily be fastened to the aviary wire.

Niger, Rape, and Poppy seeds are high in oil. Birdkeepers consider them to be tonic foods. They are expensive.

Sunflower seeds, from several sources if possible. Sunflower might well make up 30% of the seed diet by weight.

Rye. Serve it raw or cooked, white or brown. Some birds like it and others ignore it.

Peanuts and peanut butter on bread are good sources of protein and fat.

Dried Peppers. Many parrots like peppers. Consider them as a variety food or a treat.

Canary Seed. An important lovebird food.

Milo. Larger than millet, milo is often eaten by wild lovebirds.

Kibbled dog food. This is a balanced but low-fat, high-protein food supplement. Many bird breeders offer it crushed, as a source of minerals and vitamins. Read the label before you give it to your birds.

Fresh raw vegetables and fruits, including carrots, spinach, celery, dandelion, cucumber, melon, apple, orange, banana, budding twigs, grapes, figs, and corn-on-the-cob.

Eggs, hardboiled for twenty minutes, diced up with a fork, including the shell.

Mealworms can also be offered.

Now if you have only one or two birds, it would be absurd to offer everything, every day. Start with fresh water, dry seed mix, grit, and cuttlebone. Then supplement this diet with a piece of celery one day and perhaps apple on another day. Encourage your pets to taste these supplements but don't starve a bird into eating something it dislikes.

Here is a ready reference list of many of the seeds lovebirds have been known to eat. Review it briefly with the thought that the protein content of their food should be not less than 15%. Remember also that a seed which contains only 12% protein when weighed in its husk will probably contain 15% or even 20% after the hull is removed and discarded.

Lovebirds will accept many different kinds of seed, so a parrot mix, which includes a variety of seeds, large and small, is frequently offered.

Seed, including hull	Percentage of:				Carbohydrate*
	Protein	Fat	Fiber	Ash	
Rice	8	2	9	5	65
Wheat	12	2	2	2	72
Oats	12	4	12	3	58
Millet	13	2	9	4	62
Canary Seed	14	4	21	10	27
Spray Millet	15	6	11	6	51
Sunflower	15	28	29	3	17
Fennel	16	12	14	9	32
Niger	19	43	14	3	12
Rape	20	45	6	4	18
Caraway	20	17	16	7	29
Poppy	21	50	5	7	10
Sesame	21	47	5	6	19
Hemp	22	30	19	5	16
Gold of Pleasure	22	31	11	7	22
Flax	24	37	6	4	22
Peanut	28	36	3	2	18

*Carbohydrate, other than fiber

A Peach-faced Lovebird peers out of the foliage (*above*). While plants can provide the privacy that encourages breeding, lovebirds are likely to destroy them. Sometimes several pairs are kept together in the same flight (*opposite*), but some pairs may require separate housing before they will breed successfully.

GRAVEL

Wild lovebirds eat gravel, which is held in the gizzard and utilized to grind the husked seeds which are swallowed whole. The grinding action of the gravel in the gizzard is often described as equivalent to the chewing action of one's molars. This is logical; it makes sense. For centuries, all captive seedeating birds have been offered gravel.

At present, informed medical advice from veterinarians who have studied captive birds is that seedeating cage birds do not need gravel. In fact, they say, it does more harm than good. Opinion among bird keepers on this subject is not unanimous. Suffice it to say, some expert will tell you that you are doing it wrong. Perhaps you should let your birds decide.

Bear in mind that most gravel is quartz, or quartzite, or silica, or sandstone or some other mineral derived from silicon dioxide. This substance is insoluble in stomach acid. On the other hand, cuttlebone, the product of the cuttlefish (a mollusk related to the squid and the octopus) is mostly calcium carbonate. Calcium carbonate is also the main ingredient of limestone, marble, egg shells, and oyster shell. This substance is soluble in the stomach acid of a bird; thus calcium is made available for egg-shell production, bone building, and feather growth.

Care and Housing

BEHAVIOR

Lovebirds are quiet at night. They like to roost in nest boxes rather than in the open. Sleeping at night they get along well with one another, but during the day each pair is best in a cage by themselves. Many authors describe most lovebirds as "spiteful." They are not at the top of the list of good personal pets. A single, hand-raised lovebird may be a fine, gentle, friendly, trusting pet, but this is the exception, not the rule. A breeding pair will probably not tolerate any living thing within biting range. This is why the separators between pairs should be either solid or double-wired, with an inch-and-a-half gap between the mesh. To provide less will cost some poor bird a toe, or worse.

Females dominate the pair relationship. The males are usually smaller, and they do what they are told to do. Males will sometimes abuse fledglings to the point where you must take over and hand-rear the youngsters or remove the male.

The Peach-faced is probably the meanest of the readily available species, while the Nyasa is usually conceded to be the most tractable.

Your birds will probably learn to bathe, but bathing is not a big thing in their lives. They will more likely choose to sit it out in a warm, gentle rain than splash in a bath dish.

Lovebirds will eat a little at a time all day long. You should keep fresh, clean food before them at all times. They may also snooze for short periods during the day. This is perfectly normal.

A nesting pair in a walk-in flight will take possession and attack a visitor. I have had my hat knocked off by a lovebird.

Like most parrots, lovebirds love to chew and will gnaw and eventually destroy a wooden cage; therefore, strong wire-mesh cages are in order (*opposite*). Horizontal wires will allow the bird freedom of movement as it climbs up the sides and along the top of its cage. Tree branches (*above*) make ideal perches and can be fitted to most any cage or aviary. The various branch thicknesses offer lovebirds the opportunity to exercise their legs and feet.

CAGES AND AVIARIES

There is no easy answer to how to house lovebirds. First you must decide whether it will be one pair or several; whether it will be one species or several; whether you intend to go into aviculture commercially or just for fun.

Generally speaking, a single lovebird should be housed in a cage of not less than seven cubic feet. This might be 1.5 ft. high x 1.5 ft. wide x 3.0 ft. long. A second bird would need only one additional cubic foot. By this formula, a cage 2 x 2 x 2 ft. would be adequate for a compatible pair. Most species are best kept as separate pairs when they are adult, but juveniles, especially nest mates, may get along together in groups—but don't count on it.

Of course a larger cage or, better still, an aviary, which permits real flight, is great for the birds, but it doesn't always fit into a home. So you decide, and then you live with your decision. If an aviary is the way you wish to go, go slowly.

There are several things you *must* pay particular attention to, in order to benefit from the experience of others. Read this carefully, and until your own knowledge, based on your own experience, tells you otherwise, follow these guidelines. Don't re-invent the wheel.

Next: Read a book about aviary design. One good one is *Building an Aviary* by Naether and Vriends. Then closely consider these construction details:

Wire-mesh walls should be double and spaced at least one-and-one-half inches apart if they are to separate birds. Single mesh will result in lost toes and broken bills. These birds may love their mates, but it is highly unlikely that they will always be at peace with other lovebirds.

Mesh should have three-eighths-inch spacing, galvanized, since this will keep mice out. Half-inch mesh might admit a young mouse, and he would be an unwelcome pest.

Wood framing facing the birds should be covered with mesh so they cannot gnaw the wood. Ideally, outdoor aviaries should be covered with mosquito netting over the wire mesh, with a minimum of an inch and a half between the mosquito netting and the galvanized mesh. The netting will keep out those insects which might transmit diseases from wild birds. The space will reduce the risk of galvanic action between dissimilar metals, since the inside wire is

A 2 x 2 x 2 ft. cage offers sufficient room for a lovebird pair. Sheets of newspaper that line the cage floor should be changed daily.

zinc-coated steel and the outside may be copper or aluminum.

Aviary doors should be less than the full height of the flight. This is because birds bent on escaping will always try to fly over your head. If you must duck, your lovebird is more likely to remain captive.

In designing your aviary, try to get the light from the corridor where you are into the flight area where the birds are. Birds always look better when the light is coming from behind the observer. You will be able to spot trouble sooner, and you will be better able to enjoy their colors.

Try to create an entry with double, spring-loaded doors. Leave enough room between the doors so you can close one before you open the other.

If you are building outside, bury at least two feet of the wire mesh to discourage cats, dogs, rats, weasels, foxes, skunks, opossums, raccoons . . . what did I forget? They won't forget; they will be after your birds without respite.

Homemade wooden nest boxes (*above*) are welcomed by a family of Peach-faced Lovebirds. The cock perches on a dowel that is positioned just below the nestbox entrance so that he can keep an eye on things. An ideal arrangement for lovebirds (*opposite*) includes an outdoor flight attached to the side of a house or building. When opened, the windows allow easy entry into a warm room furnished with nest boxes, food, and water.

Adjacent cages should be placed with some space between them, as some lovebirds are quarrelsome and may try to bite each other while hanging on the wire; the result could be a broken or missing toe.

Leave part of the aviary roof uncovered, exposed to rain; many lovebirds which will not bathe in a bowl or a dish will enjoy bathing in the rain. Provide shade—it is possible to cook even tropical African lovebirds if you don't provide a place where they can get out of the sun.

TEMPERATURE

Lovebirds are African, but not all Africa is hot and steamy. Today in the U.S.A., lovebirds are bred in outside aviaries in Florida, Texas, and southern California. They survive an occasional mild frost so long as a box or hollow log in which they can roost is provided. You will discover that these birds will pack into a very small space at night; then they will spend the day squabbling to the extent that you could not imagine a reconciliation would ever be possible. Cold makes strange bedfellows.

So, give your lovebirds warm, dry roosting places and temperatures usually between 70 and 90 F. during the day and not more than forty degrees cooler at night. You may notice that they eat more oily seeds if it is cool at night.

Damp cold is less tolerable than dry cold, and a cold breeze is less tolerable than cold still air. On the high-temperature side, make sure that the temperature never goes over 100 F. Provide a bath, a continuous cool water spray, and shade, preferably leafy shade, to ensure that your birds don't cook. Remember that *you* caged the bird and that the responsibility for their well-being is entirely yours. It is true that a sick bird in a hospital cage will surely have a better chance of recovering at 90 F. than at 65 F., but no lovebird should be kept at 90 F. continuously.

HANDLING LOVEBIRDS

Unless you know something to the contrary, you should assume that, just as all guns are always loaded, so all lovebirds will always bite. And they can draw blood. You may be able to tame a grown lovebird; then again you may not. If you start with a nestling and hand-rear it as its mother might, you should end up with a tame and affectionate personal pet, but a lovebird is really the wrong bird for that kind of effort. It is no more difficult, but it is much more rewarding to hand-rear a cockatoo or a macaw or an African Grey, since these birds, when tame, are acknowledged to be very desirable pets. In my opinion, the lovebird is a good bird for a beginner; it is hardy, long-lived, easy to care for, inexpensive, and prolific. It is not a talker or a singer or a whistler. Its chatter is strident, not musical. Lovebird varieties are fascinating to people all over the world. There are plenty of good reasons to keep this kind of parrot—but as a tame talker, no.

There is hardly any reason to handle your lovebird. Put it in an aviary or a cage, and it will remain healthy for ten or perhaps twenty years, raising ten or more youngsters every year, but never requiring a claw clipping or a beak trimming or any other physical contact with you.

Bear in mind that a normally gentle lovebird, especially a female, may become aggressive if it has babies in the nest.

If you must handle your bird for medication or some other good reason, wear leather gloves, at least for the first time. Cup the bird in your hand so that its head is between your fingers and its beak is pointed away from anything that could be pinched or scratched.

In order to maintain the humidity necessary for successful hatching, some breeders fasten a water-filled jar to the bottom of the nest box (*above*). Holes allow moisture to penetrate the nesting material in the box. Lovebird hens are responsible for most of the incubating, so cocks (*opposite*) will frequently stand watch just outside the nest.

DISEASES & DISABILITIES

Mites, lice, and ticks can be controlled with no-pest strips *used intermittently* and with sprays available in pet shops.

Dead-in-shell losses are sometimes ascribed to low cage humidity, but I don't believe that humidity is the way to handle this problem. If the adult birds have a bath that they enjoy and use frequently, ample moisture will get into the nest via their damp feathers. Even if the male doesn't incubate the eggs, he does go into the nest box at least once in every twenty-four hours.

Aviary lovebirds are vulnerable to frostbitten feet— equatorial Africa, remember? Make sure that there is someplace in the aviary where your birds can find a warm roost.

Missing or injured toes are usually a result of fights between birds in adjacent cages. You should double-wire all cages which adjoin others occupied by hookbilled birds. A bird with a badly damaged foot has a hard time copulating, and infertile eggs will result.

Overgrown beaks and claws are unusual among lovebirds; provide cuttlebone and plenty of wood for gnawing.

Feather plucking is a vice which probably results from improper nutrition or overbreeding. If you have only one bird that always does it, get rid of that bird.

Egg-binding is usually the result of chills, overbreeding, or malnutrition. These are all your responsibility. Maintain temperatures betwen 40 and 90 F. Limit your breeders to three clutches per year; then remove your nest boxes if necessary, or better still, just reduce the length of daylight. Assure an adequate supply of a variety of foods. An egg-bound hen can usually be relieved by application of a lubricant, warmth, and water vapor.

MOLTING

Youngsters gradually get to look like their parents during perhaps'their first six months. Thereafter, that's what they look like for the remainder of their lives. Over the course of a year, feathers are lost and replaced here and there so that a normal, healthy bird never looks bedraggled. You need do nothing. If it was necessary to *clip* some wing feathers, they may remain stubs for as long as a year, but if you should *pluck* any feather, it will grow back within weeks.

Breeding

You had to wade through a lot of information before coming to this chapter, but let's face it, your birds will never breed unless everything else is right.

PAIRING

First be sure you have a pair. This isn't necessarily the easiest thing. Both sexes of the Peach-faced and the white-eye-ring birds look alike.

There are a few clues to sexing, but positive, one-hundred-percent certainty comes only from a look at the internal reproductive organs by a veterinarian who specializes in this sort of thing. Here then are the suggestions; make the most of them:

> Pairs tend to cozy up with each other.
> Males tend to feed their mates.
> Females tend to be larger than males.
> Females tend to be domineering, and they rule the roost.
> Females tend to spread their tails, while males tend to keep their tail feathers closer together.
> Females have wider spacing between their pelvic bones.

Parrots, like people, are not necessarily "normal." Sometimes two males or two females will become attracted to each other. In a case like this, watch the nest. Males don't carry nest materials in the typical lovebird fashion, and males don't lay eggs. If two lovebirds lay ten infertile eggs in the same nest, you can be pretty sure you

Eggs are laid approximately every other day until there are about four or five in the clutch (*above*). Newborn lovebirds, one and three days old (*below*), should be left to the care of their parents. Do not interfere with the brood except to occasionally inspect the nest box.

Eye slits, ear openings, and nostrils are clearly visible on this one-week-old lovebird chick (above). In a few days, its eyes will fully open, and in a few weeks, feathers will begin to emerge amidst the downy plumage (*below*).

have a pair of females. Do not take this bond too seriously; they may be separated, and new mates may be provided.

It is sad but true that the lovebird species in which the sexes differ are not commonly available. These, as I mentioned elsewhere, are the Gray-headed, Black-winged, Red-faced, and Black-collared. The remainder of the genus *Agapornis* make up ninety-nine percent of the lovebirds in captivity; these, the Peach-faced and the four with white eye rings, are the only ones that most fanciers ever get to see. In case you have forgotten the names of the four with white eye rings, they are Fischer's, Masked, Black-cheeked, and Nyasa.

If you get involved in breeding color varieties, you will find that some are sex-linked, so that it is sometimes possible to relate the color to sex. If it were really easy, everyone would be doing it. That is the challenge of aviculture.

CHOOSING BREEDERS

Get the best quality you can afford. Buy from an established pet shop or a recognized breeder. Look for solid, fully-feathered, alert, tight-feathered, active, clean birds. Avoid the droopers, sleepers, and sneezers; avoid puffy, dirty, bumble-footed, split-billed, skinny, patchily feathered, weepy-eyed, or wet-vented birds.

Choose for your first pair an inexpensive variety. Start slowly: just one pair, a large cage, and two nestboxes. Keep your bird-breeding hobby simple, to avoid tears.

AGE TO BREED

This is not the last word about a controversial subject. Some breeders feel that they get better babies from parents that are not bred until they are two years old. Other breeders let nature take its course, and when they do, they find that some lovebirds start nesting about as soon as they come into full color, perhaps at six months of age. Does this lead to infertile eggs and egg binding and deserted nests and undersized or sickly babies? Opinions differ, and I don't know.

Certainly no one in Africa keeps the young birds segregated by sexes until they are a certain age. One thing we do know is that it is very difficult to determine the sex of most lovebirds, and it is also something of a bother to keep

Affectionate behavior between two lovebirds does not mean that they are a true (male and female) pair.

males separate from females. Of course, you can keep your birds from breeding by providing less than twelve hours of light daily and by not furnishing nest boxes; but I think this is a mistake because many lovebirds will naturally prefer to roost in a nestbox.

NESTS

Your birds will likely prefer to nest in something that resembles their childhood home. This may seem like a trite statement, but it may well make the difference between having two caged lovebirds and having a breeding pair and a nest box full of youngsters. A well-furnished cage or aviary will have *at least* one nest box *for every bird*. Yes, that's right: two per pair, minimum, at least until the birds have had an opportunity to choose for themselves. You should not decide to remove an unused box until at least two breeding campaigns have been completed. You may discover that your birds will leave that first nestbox to their first brood and that the second clutch of eggs will be laid in the other box. Or, they may try to kick out the first brood—with shed feathers, shed blood, and perhaps death resulting. These birds have their own lifestyle.

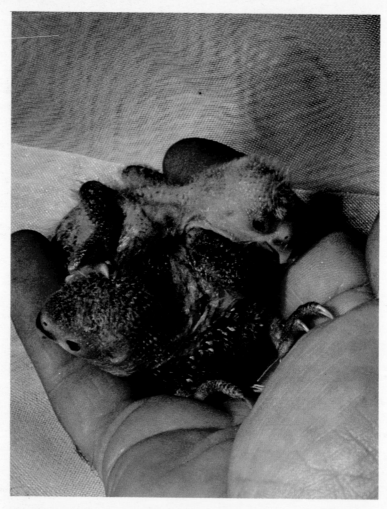

These babies are only forty-eight hours apart in age (*above*). In about three weeks, it will be impossible to tell which is the older of the two. Pin feathers, or prickles, are noticeable on this youngster (*opposite, above*), and feather development is well under way on this juvenile (*opposite, below*).

We call them lovebirds, but if they could talk, they might well admit to something more cruel and violent. Many experienced lovebird fanciers call breeding lovebirds spiteful. Bear in mind that while an individual bird, hand-reared and thoughtfully tamed, may well be your best hook-billed pet, birds breeding in a large cage or an aviary are altogether another matter.

Your birds will probably choose a nest box like the one they hatched in. If they came out of a box, you may be unsuccessful offering a hollow log or cardboard tube or wicker basket. If you don't know where your birds were raised, assume that it was a conventional lovebird box; this is what you should offer.

A hollow log, about eight to twelve inches in diameter and perhaps two feet long, may stimulate a pair to breed. If it has a natural hole in its side, good. If not, you might bore one, about an inch and a half to two inches in diameter. Close off the ends of the log with flat boards and stand or hang it as high in the aviary as you can. A cupful or two of punky wood in the cavity is a good start for a nest,

Nest boxes have been attached to the outside of the wire to permit inspection by the keeper. A back door unfastens so that the observer can check the nest without having to enter the flight itself.

In the wild lovebirds breed in small colonies, so in captivity several compatible pairs will sometimes be housed together in the same flight. Here the nest boxes have been fastened inside the aviary.

according to some authorities, but don't neglect to furnish an adequate supply of fresh twigs and vines for your birds to pulverize as well. A wicker nest basket which remained in an aviary once occupied by finches was quickly demolished by a pair of Peach-faced Lovebirds while this book was being written. Every shred was carried to the nest box, and the basket ended up as a cotton-soft cup in the bottom of the cavity. That took a lot of chewing.

Breeders of budgies use a nestbox with a removable dish-shaped board. It is sometimes called a "concave" or "concave bottom." This tends to keep the eggs from rolling into the corners of a square nestbox, where they will perish due to lack of incubating warmth. This is necessary for budgies, since they do not create a nest lining, but it is not especially important for lovebirds. If your ready-built nest box has a concave, don't discard it, but if it lacks one, don't worry.

When you put a nest box or a hollow log into a lovebird aviary, sometimes the birds will enter it within minutes

The cock regurgitates partially digested food and feeds it to the hen as part of courtship ritual (*above*). In a few days, this Peach-faced youngster will fledge (*opposite, above*), although its parents may continue to feed it even after it has left the nest. A hungry chick (*opposite, below*) awaits its next meal. Its parents have left the nest box for food and some exercise.

and sometimes they will ignore it for months and then fill it with brood after brood of babies. Should the opening face the light? Opinions differ, but most breeders agree that the bottom of the cavity should be dark.

If offered a choice, aviary lovebirds will favor a high nestbox over one located near the floor. Obviously, birds in cages have less choice, but when all the other conditions are right, they will do everything in their power to nest and raise their young.

Should you build or buy your nest boxes? I advise you to buy at least one or two of the standard, commercially available boxes before making any by yourself.

You will find that a box 5.5 x 6.0 x 7.0 in. high, with an entry hole 2 in. in diameter and a perch 3 in. long and five-sixteenths inch in diameter, is just fine for Peach-faced lovebirds and the other readily available varieties, provided the nest box is located inside a building.

The height of 7 in. is a minimum. An additional inch or two or three of height may be more desirable. A deeper nestbox might well be furnished with a perch which extends *into* the nestbox about 2.5 in., so that the nesting adult can reach the hole without having to jump. Really deep nestboxes (over 10 in.) need inside ladders of one-half-inch wire mesh, especially for the youngsters.

The base of 5.5 x 6.0 in. is adequate for four or five babies. They seem to thrive in closeness. Perhaps the body heat of the first hatchling helps to warm its younger siblings. Actually, during the first ten days or so of a lovebird's life, it is somewhat reptilian in appearance and in its metabolism. It needs warmth from an external source to survive and digest its food. You will discover that chicks ten days or older do maintain warmth and keep their younger nest mates warm without any daytime help from the parents. This is convenient because by ten days of age the appetite of a baby lovebird requires that both parents spend time foraging to keep its crop filled. Of course, with an adequate supply of good food and water, this ceases to be a problem—but the habits of centuries are built-in, and that is the way it is.

So then, the size of the conventional nest box ties in with the habits and metabolism of the birds. Don't start out by inventing a new design.

Your lovebirds will have a good deal of time to spend fooling around. Caged birds are not chased by predators or obliged to fly long distances for water or nest sites. Food is furnished in abundance, almost within walking distance.

Of course some "spare" time is taken up with bickering, and they are good at that. Additional time is taken for sitting close to each other and preening feathers. The rest of their spare time is sometimes employed chewing wooden supports and perches and nest boxes.

Don't be surprised if a couple of lovebirds completely disintegrate their nest box. They are capable of grinding up everything but the screws or nails with which it was fastened. Perhaps if your nest boxes are valuable and room permits, you could provide some fresh apple or maple or willow twigs for them to work over. They might even eat the buds, and the bark could end up in a nest, but regardless, you will have saved a nest box. Try tying a bundle of twigs to the side or top of the enclosure, the higher the better.

Assume the worst: that you know you have a pair, but they refuse to enter the nest box. First, make sure they don't roost in it at night—take a quiet peek after the lights have gone out. If they do use it as a roost, but refuse to nest, something else is wrong. Search for things such as malnutrition, crowding, less than twelve hours of daylight, distractions, lack of nest-making materials, or anything else you can think of. If nothing works, you might try stuffing the nest box with a loose handful of fresh honeysuckle vines. Let them hang out of the nestbox hole. The birds will work over those leaves and tendrils; first outside and eventually inside the box. Good luck!

If you did get one good nestful of babies and then no more, it is perhaps a matter of crowding. You may have to remove those young birds as soon as they can care for themselves before the parents will do any more breeding.

THE BREEDING CYCLE

Assume you have a pair of sexually mature birds (over six months of age). Ideally, you should isolate them from all other birds and provide them with *two* nest boxes and some fresh twigs and vines to make their nest lining. If conditions of nutrition, temperature, humidity, light, and

Newborn lovebirds are covered with a yellowish down (Fischer's—*above*). By the time the feathers emerge, the chicks have the greenish gray of a second down coat (Peach-faced—*opposite*), which gives way to the green of the juvenile plumage.

Lovebird eggs are sometimes a bit dirty, but always white. Clutches typically consist of four or five eggs, rarely six.

isolation from disturbing influences are right, your birds will pair up, copulate, build a nest within a nest box and raise a family. The timetable is about like this:

Courtship. Male regurgitates food from his crop to feed female. Copulation is often relatively lengthy and repeated several times each day for several days. The nest box is selected and shredded twigs and bark are brought in and arranged in the bottom.

Egg-laying. One egg is laid every other day or so until there are about five, never more than six. Incubation usually starts after the second egg is laid.

Incubation. Eggs are incubated for twenty-one to twenty-three days and then hatch in the order in which they were laid.

Brooding. Youngsters develop in the nest box for five or six weeks. Then they gradually spend more time outside it during the day. At night they continue to roost in the nest box unless evicted by the parents (this is why some breeders provide two boxes for each pair of adult birds).

This is an *actual log* of Peach-faced Lovebirds going through a breeding cycle, beginning on July 16th.

7/16—Male regurgitates food and feeds his mate
7/17—Copulation and nest building
7/19—First egg laid on shredded bark
7/20—More nest materials added
7/22—Second egg laid, intermittent incubation
7/25—Third egg, hen in nest full time
7/28—Four eggs (no inspection on 7/27, so this egg may have been laid that day)
7/29—Incubation continues
8/12—First egg pipped
8/13—First egg hatched
8/16—Second egg hatched
8/18—Three chicks and one egg
8/24—Three downy chicks. Last egg examined; it proved infertile and was removed
9/2—Chicks in pin feathers, tails out one-quarter inch and showing color
9/14—Largest chick looking out nest-box hole
9/19—First chick leaving nest for short periods during day. All chicks plus parents in nest box at night.
9/30—All chicks flying and feeding themselves, but continuing to beg food from parents
10/20—Adult birds start a new nest

BANDS

Many cage birds are routinely banded for identification. This is useful for controlled breeding and for exhibition. Pigeon keepers have been doing it for centuries, and, of course, many finches and canaries and budgies are also permanently banded soon after they hatch. Some canary hens will object, to the extent of tearing off these bands from their babies or even kicking the babies out of the nest. With lovebirds, the bands are sometimes crushed in an attempt to remove them, and the babies' feet are thereby injured. After you have raised a few dozen lovebirds, you may wish to experiment with permanent metal bands on some babies, or you may wish to try open rings which can be clamped on adult birds to aid in recognizing pairs in an

Nest boxes of a design readily accepted by lovebirds (*above*). At least two per pair should be fastened to the wire of breeding flights (*opposite, below*). The Masked Lovebirds (*opposite, above*), about to leave their nest box, have the markings of adults, but the colors are duller.

aviary. The advantage to a breeder of having a banded bird is tremendous but not without some risk. Open metal rings clamped on adult birds are much less risky than closed rings slipped on babies. On lovebirds plastic rings will usually be chewed off before the day is over.

GOING COMMERCIAL

The best advice, and the hardest to accept, is *don't do it.* If you want to keep lovebirds, this is fine. If you want to breed lovebirds, this is great. If you want to sell your surplus, this is okay too. If you want to make money by breeding lovebirds, you must be either ignorant of the facts or out of your mind.

Remember that the *wholesale price* is much lower than the retail, pet-shop price. The mark-up is necessary to cover transportation, losses, taxes, advertising, and a small profit at each of the steps between the egg and the purchaser. If demand for lovebirds should suddenly increase tremendously—and this is very unlikely—the established commercial breeders in Florida, Texas, and southern California with their enormous aviaries could, within the year, saturate the market while you were still getting started. An old expression worth repeating here is "Shoemaker, stick to your last."

Summary of Things You Should Do to Breed Lovebirds

Be patient.

Start with an "easy" species, such as the Peach-faced.

Be sure that you have a male-and-female pair, then leave them together.

Isolate the pair in the largest enclosure you can afford. A three-foot-long cage is the minimum.

Provide a wide variety of high-quality, fresh food and water. Offer fresh vegetables and fruits even if they aren't eaten at first.

Provide at least one nest box, preferably two.

Ensure twelve hours of light daily, on a regular, timed basis.

Furnish a variety of fresh twigs and rootlets for nest building. Honeysuckle, forsythia, birch, and willow are all acceptable. Avoid evergreens since the sticky sap will cause trouble.

Wild lovebirds travel in flocks, but they tend to nest alone, so don't crowd two breeding pairs into one small cage. You will get more production from one uncrowded pair than from two pairs that are constantly bickering or competing for mates, nests, perches, food, or whatever.

Your birds are willful, and they will notice and favor things you never thought of. Let them make choices, and they will reward you with large broods of healthy babies. For examples of the choices you should offer, consider: two nest boxes—one facing the light and the other with the opening away from the light; variety of foods, and cuttlebone, vegetables and fruit, hardboiled egg and insects. Fresh corn, peas-in-the-pod, and half-ripe grass seeds are also relished.

Most wild lovebirds are not found in areas with freezing temperatures (the exception is *A. taranta*). Keep them over 40 F. and under 90 F. The ideal temperature is probably about 70 to 75 F. for all species.

Not all wild lovebirds bathe frequently, but they all do enjoy water, and they certainly drink a goodly amount of fresh, clean, cool water. This is easy to provide, and it does make a difference.

Give the birds privacy. Don't molest or even hover over them. They manage better when left alone.

Avoid flashing lights, noise, rattling of cages, etc., especially at night.

Don't band the first few nestlings; the risk outweighs any advantage.

Be patient.

Among the lovebirds without eye rings are the Peach-faced (*above*) and the Gray-headed (*opposite*). Unlike the Peach-faced, however, the other species without eye rings are sexually dimorphic. Gray-headed hens lack the gray of the cocks.

Lovebirds are popular cage and aviary birds because they are relatively inexpensive, easy to feed, resistant to most diseases, and they can be found in a variety of colors.

More About Lovebirds

No one book on this subject will ever satisfy everyone. Some readers want a how-to-do-it approach, others prefer more natural history and behavior, and still others are so far advanced that they need a book on just color varieties. Here is a selection of titles with the contents briefly described. Unless you are a book collector, it would be wasteful to own all of them.

Parrots of the World by Forshaw and Cooper. This is *the* source book for parrot keepers seeking to know about distribution, reproduction in the wild, food, and behavior. Every species of parrot in the world is described. There are 584 pages of distribution maps and full-color paintings. Forshaw and Cooper costs a lot of money, but when you consider that there are so many large pages of solid facts "with no commercial interruptions," this book is most reasonably priced. Certainly every author of parrot literature relies on Forshaw and Cooper.

Parrots and Related Birds by Bates and Busenbark is now in its third edition. It was written by bird keepers, for bird keepers. There are 543 pages about the care, description, and handling of parrots in aviculture.

Parrots and Parrot-like Birds by the 12th Duke of Bedford is an accounting by a British nobleman of his experience with birds in his unheated aviaries. Of course, it is more useful for British aviary keepers than for Americans who tend to keep their birds in more temperate and sheltered accommodations.

Dutch Blue Peach-faced Lovebirds. The name of this color variety is not an attempt to describe the shade of color; instead, "Dutch" refers to the first occurrence of the mutation in Holland, and "Blue" means that the yellow pigment is diminished.

The inhabitants of this aviary are a Masked Lovebird, a Peach-faced, and a hybrid of Masked and Peach-faced.

Breeding Lovebirds by Silva and Kotlar is a 93-page primer fully illustrated with good sharp photos, many of which are in color.

All About Lovebirds by Soderberg is based on his widely read *Foreign Birds for Cage and Aviary*; this is a comprehensive and inexpensive 96-page book.

Encyclopedia of Lovebirds by Vriends is a 256-page hardcover book. The first half covers the basics of care and breeding, and the remainder of the book describes each of the varieties. The book also includes chapters on parrotlets, hanging parrots, and fig parrots. Vriends also devotes several pages to hybrids.

Lovebirds and Their Color Mutations by Hayward is a hardcover book of 108 pages written and published in Great Britain. The genetics section contains over 60 pages of details. For example, there is an illustration to assist in "Predicting the color variety of Peach-faced hatchlings by examining their eyes and bills."

The T.F.H. Book of Lovebirds by Radtke is a 77-page, large-format book. It is illustrated with excellent photos entirely in color. All the wild forms and many of the color varieties are shown. The pictures are not just good—they are superb.

Encyclopedia of Cage and Aviary Birds by Rogers is not a lovebird book, but it does contain a useful section on this genus. Rogers is a highly respected British author.

Lovebirds and Related Parrots by Smith is a 180-page book, packed with a tremendous amount of useful detail. Smith tells us a great deal about lovebird behavior, and his suggestions for care and breeding are excellent.

*Published by T.F.H. Publications.

A Technician's View of Handling Birds and Performing Routine Physical Exams

Missy Meers, Miki Roche,
Maggie Parhm, and Susan Gibson
Animal Health Technicians
at Atlanta Animal Hospital, Dunwoody, Georgia

Pet birds are not difficult to handle. However, they are easily injured and can cause a great deal of pain and injury to the inexperienced handler. Before taking a bird out of its cage, cut off escape routes by closing doors and windows. Birds adapt slowly to changes in light, so turning out room lights should make the bird easy to catch. Small birds such as Budgerigars can be caught bare-handed and held in the palm of your hand, holding the head either between thumb and forefinger or between forefinger and middle finger. By cupping your hand you can both support its back and also hold its wings.

Larger birds may be caught with gloves or a towel. Many birds become glove-shy while in quarantine—a towel may work better. Wrap the bird in the towel, holding the back of its head through the towel. Let it chew contentedly at the fabric to take its mind off what you are doing. Wings or feet are easy to unwrap for feather-trims or

Tame birds (*above*) are easy to handle, especially when they need medical attention. While holding a lovebird (*opposite*), be careful to control its head with your thumb and forefinger—a bite on the cuticle can be very painful.

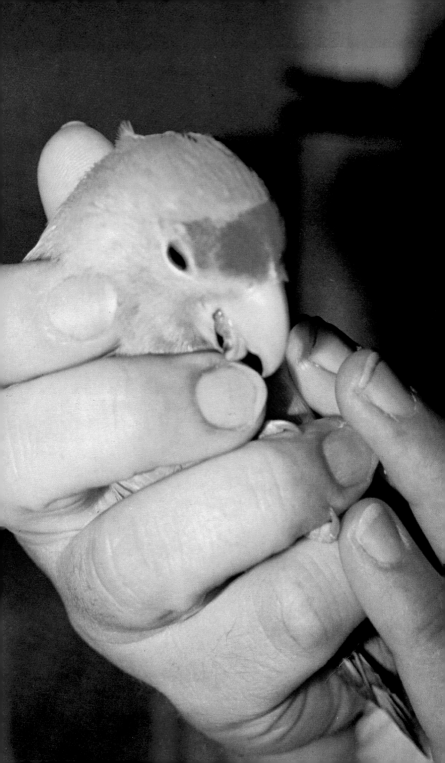

nail-trims. Although some birds use their beaks aggressively (storks, particularly, aim to put your eyes out), birds of prey such as hawks defend themselves with their feet and can easily pierce your wrist with their talons—control their feet first.

Birds have no diaphragm. If you apply pressure to the breast (keel bone) and inhibit thoracic movement, a bird may rapidly asphyxiate. Birds also have an unusual breathing system composed of lungs and air sacs—they do not cough or sneeze well. After giving a bird medicine, give it its head so it can shake out any excess liquid, or it may choke or inhale the medicine.

If a bird escapes your hold, first check that all exits are closed, then turn off the lights. The bird will generally fly to the floor or a convenient perch. Be careful of back-lit glass such as a window into the next room, as the bird may fly toward the light and hit the window glass. A bird on a hard-to-reach perch may step onto a stick placed before its legs. We recommend against using nets, as it is easy for a bird tangled in a net to break a wing or leg.

After obtaining a complete history of the bird's nutrition, management, and problems, observe the bird in its cage. Look for fluffed feathers, tail fluking (tail lifting to assist breathing, a sign of dyspnea), nasal or ocular discharge, unusual number or character of droppings, lameness or other postural abnormalities, lethargy, and so forth. Catch the bird and take its temperature before it gets excited and its body temperature rises. Lift the tail to expose the vent and insert the thermometer no more than about 1 cm. Pediatric rectal thermometers work well. A normal bird's temperature is more than 39°C. (103°F.) Add 1° if the bird is excited. There are a few species with a different temperature range, but you are unlikely to encounter them in practice—a healthy penguin may have a temperature of 43°C. (110°F.). An excited macaw may blush, so don't worry if its cheeks turn red.

If feathers are dull and lifeless, the bird may have a nutritional deficiency. Check the "wing-pits" for small red or dark feather mites. In a feather plucker, note the location of plucked feathers. If feathers have been plucked from the back of the head and neck, another bird is probably doing the plucking. Check the eyes, using an ophthalmoscope if necessary. Touch the beak to get the bird to open its mouth and check for ulcers or scabs. Check the legs and cere for crusty, honey-combed skin which may be due to scaly-leg mites (verify with a microscope). Feel the crop and see if it is empty or full to gauge whether the bird has just eaten and to check for foreign bodies in the crop. Feel the keel bone—the muscle should be level with the edge of the keel. Atrophy indicates weight loss. Check for lumps and bumps. The uropygial, or preen, gland on top of the tail base can become impacted like a dog's anal glands and may need to be expressed. In listening to the heart and lungs use a stethoscope with a rubber ring to avoid background sound of feathers rubbing on the stethoscope. When a bird is standing, its heart is located approximately between its legs. Listen to both left and right sides of the chest and be alert for arrhythmias. The lungs are attached to the dorsal ribs—listen along the back. Listen further caudally to the air sacs. Admittedly the veterinarian is going to be doing the physical exam on most clients' birds. However, you will be helping, and you will probably be examining hospitalized birds daily. Your ability to perform a competent physical exam on a bird will be of considerable value to your hospital.

Average Avian Weights

Hummingbirds	2.4–5 gm.
Mannikins	5–11gm.
Java Sparrow	24–30 gm.
Canary	18–38 gm.
House Sparrow	27 gm.
Budgerigar	35–60 gm.
Masked Lovebird	62 gm.
Fischer's Lovebird	55–70 gm.
Glossy Starling	80 gm.
Blue-crowned Conure	92 gm.
Ringneck Parakeet	155 gm.
Greater Indian Hill Mynah	180–260 gm.
Domestic Pigeon	240–300 gm.
Crow	340 gm.
African Grey Parrot	360 gm.

This chart is very sketchy, as little work has been done on average weights in normal birds.

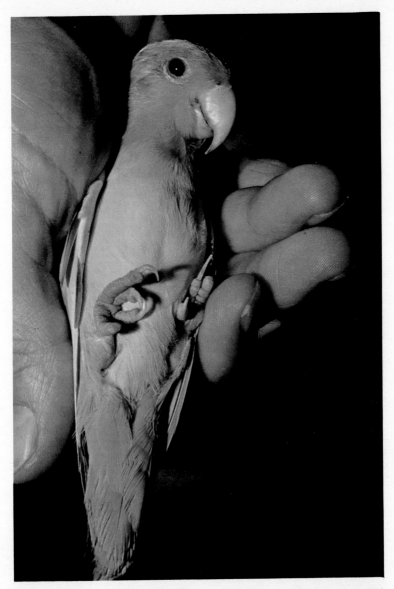

The condition of a bird's plumage is important not only in terms of appearance but also with regard to flight (*opposite, above*). As your pet lovebird spreads its wings (*opposite, below*), notice if there are any feather mites, bald patches, or evidence of feather plucking. By holding a tame lovebird in this manner, one can check the bird's breast, legs, and feet (*above*).

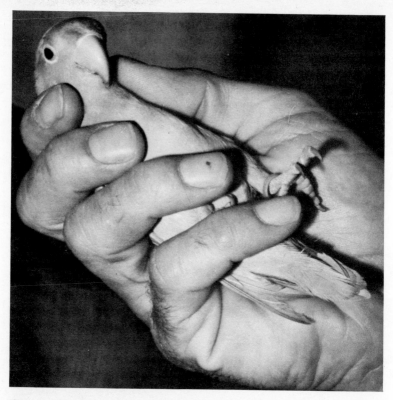

This is the proper way to hold a bird for examination. Grasp the bird with a cupped hand and hold it securely on its back.

Weigh each bird accurately. Weight is an important part of the base-line data. A scale with a weighing basket (Ohaus Scale Corp., Florham Park, New Jersey) works best. Tape up the holes to keep the bird calm and to prevent it from hooking its beak or claws in the holes. An inaccurate weight is not worth taking with an animal that weighs as little as most birds. Hospitalized birds, particularly if they are not eating and are being tubefed, should probably be weighed daily to assess their recovery. Try to weigh at the same time each day, before feeding.

None of the procedures discussed above should take any longer in a bird than they would in a dog or cat, and they are just as critical to proper care in birds as in any other animals.

Chart #1 Avian History Form

I. History
   A. Identification

   _____ Name _____ Age _____ Sex _____ Species _____

   Color _____ Weight

   B. Symptoms
      1. Major complaint _____
      2. Duration _____
      3. Appetite _____ Normal _____ Reduced _____ Anorexia
      4. Dropping
         a. Appearance _____ Dark with white center _____ Light with white scattered
            _____ Other
         b. Number _____ < 25 _____ 25 to 50 _____ > 50
         c. Consistency _____ firm _____ soft
      5. Regurgitation _____ yes _____ no
      6. Water consumption _____ Decreased _____ Normal _____ Increased
      7. Activity _____ Decreased _____ Normal _____ Increased
      8. Respiration _____ sneezing or coughing _____ tail fluking
            _____ open mouth breathing
            _____ wheezing _____ increased rate
      9. Prior illness and medication _____

   C. Environment
      1. Cage and location
         _____ new cage   _____ excessive sunlight
         _____ new cage location   _____ presence of mirror
         _____ drafts (air-conditioning & heating) _____ cage sanitation
         _____ paint chipped from cage   _____ destruction of toys
                                                        — too many toys
      2. Aerosol use
         _____ insecticides _____ paint fumes _____ other
      3. Duration of ownership _____
         Where purchased _____
      4. Other family pets _____
      5. Feed and Minerals
         Type _____
         Amount feed _____
         Location of feeder _____
         Feed additives _____ Codliver oil _____ Vitamins _____ Treats
                        _____ Calcium   _____ Greens   _____ Other
                        _____ Iodine   _____ Fruits
         Feed freshness _____
      6. Water
         How often replaced _____ Location _____
         Water sanitation _____
         Watering vehicle _____ Other _____

As a bird keeper, it is wise to keep records of your lovebirds' health in case you are ever required to fill out forms like these. Such information is vitally important, especially to those who diagnose avian diseases and disorders.

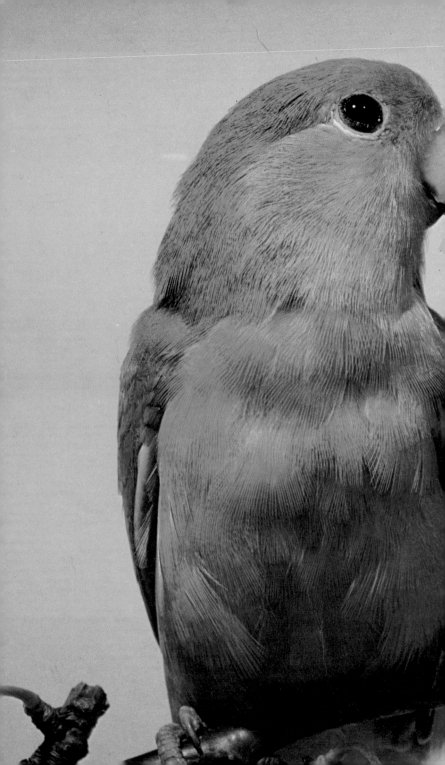